D1309326

HEINEMANN
Profiles

Henry Ford

An Unauthorized Biography

John Malam

Heinemann Library
Chicago, Illinois

© 2001 Reed Educational & Professional Publishing
Published by Heinemann Library,
an imprint of Reed Educational & Professional Publishing,
Chicago, Illinois
Customer Service 888-454-2279
Visit our website at www.heinemannlibrary.com

Produced for Heinemann Library by Discovery Books Limited
Edited by Rosemary Williams
Designed by Ian Winton
Originated by Dot Gradations
Printed and bound in Hong Kong

05 04 03 02 01
10 9 8 7 6 5 4 3 2 1

Library of Congress Cataloging-in-Publication Data
Malam, John, 1957-
  Henry Ford / John Malam
    p. cm. – (Heinemann profiles)
  Includes bibliographical references and index.
  ISBN 1-58810-058-8 (library binding)
  1. Ford, Henry, 1863-1947--Juvenile literature. 2. Automobile industry and trade--United States--Biography--Juvenile literature. 3. Industrialists--United States--Biography--Juvenile literature. [1. Ford, Henry, 1863-1947. 2. Automobile industry and trade--Biography. 3 Industrialists.] I. Title. II. Series.

HD9710.U52 F66543 2001
338.7'6292'092--dc21
[B]   00-063271

Acknowledgments
The author and publishers are grateful to the following for permission to reproduce copyright material: Science Museum/Science & Society Picture Library, p. 14; Peter Newark's American Pictures, p. 25; Bettman/Corbis, p. 26. All other photographs reproduced from the collections of the Henry Ford Museum & Greenfield Village and from Ford Motor Company, UK.

Every effort has been made to contact copyright holders of any material reproduced in this book. Any omissions will be rectified in subsequent printings if notice is given to the publisher.

This is an unauthorized biography. The subject has not sponsored or endorsed this book.

Some words are shown in bold, **like this.** You can find out what they mean by looking in the glossary.

CONTENTS

WHO WAS HENRY FORD?

As we look back through the centuries, very few people can claim to have drastically changed the world in which we live today. Yet when it comes to transportation, one person has influenced the lives of millions of people. His name was Henry Ford, and this is his story.

Of the many machines we use to travel, it is the automobile that has given us the freedom to cross land quickly, cheaply, safely and comfortably. The automobile was invented in the nineteenth century and revolutionized personal and public transportation in the twentieth century. Henry Ford, more than any other person, was the leader of that revolution.

Henry Ford (1863–1947), shown in the first official Ford Motor Company portrait in 1904.

Birth of the motor car

Henry Ford was not the inventor of the motor car. In 1886, Karl Benz (1844–1929), a German **engineer, registered** a design for a three-wheeled vehicle. Although motor vehicles had been built before then, Benz's design proved to be the best. The motor car was born, and with it came the beginnings of an industry that changed the world.

Ford cars were among the first mass-produced motor vehicles in the world.

A GRAND IDEA

From simple beginnings as a farm boy in Michigan, Henry Ford grew to become one of the world's wealthiest people. He was not to be a humble farmer like his ancestors. Instead, his **destiny** lay in the new **technology** of his day—the automobile— and in a grand idea. Ford wanted to build cars that ordinary people could afford.

Ford sensed that the automobile would change people's lives for the better. However, for that to happen he had to find a way of building cars quickly and cheaply. That meant changing the way the **manufacturing industry** worked.

What Ford created was far more than a cheap car for the masses. He brought the brand-new **automobile industry** from backyard workshops to international business success. To this day, the Ford Motor Company, which Ford established in 1903, is still one of the world's leading car manufacturers.

FAREWELL IRELAND, HELLO AMERICA

Henry Ford's story begins not in America but in Ireland. During the first half of the 1800s the Fords were farmers at Ballinascarty, County Cork. It was here that Henry Ford's grandfather, John Ford, worked. Life was hard for the farmers of Ireland, but in the 1840s a disaster struck. In 1846, a fungus called blight attacked their potato crops, a main source of nutrition. Once the crop was infected, nothing could be done to save the plants, and so they rotted in the fields. The outbreak lasted three years, and thousands of Irish families were forced to leave the land or face starvation. The Great Potato Famine, as it came to be known, was a time of poverty and hardship in Ireland.

Henry Ford's father was William Ford (1826–1905).

Among the people affected by the famine were John Ford and his family. They decided to **emigrate** to America to begin a new, and hopefully better, life. And so, in 1847, John Ford, his elderly mother, his wife, Thomasina, and their seven children went to Cork, the nearest seaport on the Atlantic coast. There they boarded an emigration ship.

Henry Ford was born in a clapboard farmhouse in Dearborn, Michigan.

A NEW HOME

The Fords sailed to Canada and then traveled south into the United States. They finally reached Michigan in 1848. At the settlement of Dearbornville—which later became Dearborn—the family bought land and set about clearing the brush.

HENRY FORD IS BORN

The Ford family settled comfortably in Michigan. In 1861, John Ford's son, William, married Mary Litogot, the foster daughter of a neighboring family. William was 35, Mary was 22. On the morning of July 30, 1863, Mary gave birth to a son. They named him Henry. He was born during the **Civil War** (1861–65), when the country was torn apart by a conflict that would change the course of its future. Little did his family know that Henry would one day change the course of his country's future, too.

"The first thing I remember in my life is my father taking my brother and myself to see a bird's nest … I remember the nest with four eggs and also the bird and hearing it sing."

Henry Ford

Raised on a Farm

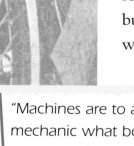

Henry Ford spent his childhood on his parents' 90-acre (36 hectare) farm, where they grew wheat, oats, apples, and peaches and raised cows, pigs, and sheep. As the oldest child of six, Henry was expected to help on the farm. But he showed little interest in the work, and would sometimes refuse to do a job. A stubborn and rebellious child, Henry preferred the excitement of Detroit, with all the din of the riverfront machinery. He had seen the city during the family's shopping trips.

> "... considering the results, there was too much work on the place."
>
> Henry Ford's recollections of life on his father's farm

An interest in mechanics

When Henry was seven, he went to Dearborn's only school, where he showed a talent for mathematics but not for English. Another talent was emerging as well—he was starting to show an interest in machines. Henry became fascinated by clocks and watches. With a set of tiny tools he'd made himself, he learned how to take their complicated **mechanisms** apart, fix them if they were broken, then reassemble them. His mother called him "her born mechanic."

> "Machines are to a mechanic what books are to a writer. He gets ideas from them, and if he has any brains, he applies those ideas."
>
> Henry Ford

1876: GRIEF AND INSPIRATION

Two events occurred in 1876 that influenced the young Ford. In March, his beloved mother died. Her death was a great blow to him. For the rest of his life, Henry remembered the lessons she had taught him. It was his mother who had encouraged him never to give up, never to pity himself if things went wrong, and to show patience and courage when doing jobs he might not like. In old age, when asked to explain his business success, Henry replied, "I have tried to live my life as my mother would have wished."

The second major event of 1876 came in mid-summer, when Henry saw a **steam engine** moving under its own power along a dirt road. It was the first time Henry had seen a vehicle moving without the aid of horses to pull it, and the experience filled his young head with ideas. When, years later, he recalled that July day, he said:, ". . . it was that engine that took me into **automotive transportation**."

Henry Ford's mother, Mary Litogot Ford (1839–1876).

Starting Work

"Automotive transportation," as Henry referred to it, was the dream of many **engineers.** The nineteenth century had already given rise to the steam locomotive, the steam ship, and the bicycle. Inventors in Belgium, France, and Germany had already begun to experiment with **"horseless carriages."** The French called them **"automobiles."**

Henry Ford, at about seventeen, when he was an apprentice engineer in Detroit.

It was against this background of technological progress that Henry Ford's career developed. During the late 1800s, changes in the way products were manufactured were transforming the way people did business in America and Europe. Ford had every intention of becoming involved with the opportunities these changes offered.

He made a decision: he would leave school as soon as he

could and train to be an engineer. In December 1879, sixteen-year-old Henry left the family farm at Dearborn and walked nine miles to the industrial city of Detroit to begin work at the engineering firm of James F. Flower & Brothers.

A HEAD FOR BUSINESS

Henry trained for four years to become an engineer, which seemed like forever to him. Not happy to stay long in any one job, Henry moved to other companies in Detroit so that he could learn more about engineering. As an **apprentice,** Henry earned little money, so in the evenings he worked as a watch-repairer. This gave him the idea of starting his own watch-making business. Henry wanted to make watches that everyone could afford. However, he estimated that to make a watch inexpensive enough for everyone to afford, he would need to produce 2,000 a day—more than half a million a year! So Henry soon gave up the idea. How could he possibly hope to sell so many watches? Even though Henry was not yet twenty, he had already started to think about **mass production**, an entirely new method of working.

"In the long run, people are going to buy the cheapest and best article—no matter where it's made."

Henry Ford

BACK ON THE FARM

When his **apprenticeship** was over, Henry could call himself an **engineer.** However, instead of looking for a job in Detroit, he returned to Dearborn and the family farm. In the peace of the countryside Henry could think about his future and how he could put his new-found engineering knowledge to good use. It wasn't long before he was called upon to use his skill with machinery.

A neighbor had bought a small **steam engine** to help in jobs around his farm. It could do the work of several people and horses, and Henry learned how it worked and how to operate it. The summer of 1882 was a happy one as Henry traveled from farm to farm taking the portable steam engine to help his neighbors.

A FAMILY MAN

Henry Ford met Clara Bryant, his future wife, on New Year's Day 1885. He fell in love with her immediately. Clara was eighteen, and he made little impression on her then, but when they met again a year later, she found that Henry was not like the other young men who lived in the area. While those men were interested in everyday things, Henry Ford was a sensible, serious fellow with lots of practical ideas. Clara grew to like him.

Henry's father, William, must have thought his son had returned to Dearborn to settle down as a farmer. In 1886, William gave Henry 80 acres (32 hectares) of uncleared woodland. Henry could cut down the trees, clear the land, and farm it. Henry's beloved steam engines would make the hard work so much easier. The history of transportation would have been very different if Henry had become a farmer, but luckily, he didn't.

Clara Bryant Ford in 1888.

Henry and Clara were married on April 11, 1888. Henry was almost 25. Clara came from a farming family and probably thought she was marrying a farmer. But Henry's interest in machines and **technology** made him stand apart from ordinary farmers.

The engine that sparked an idea

Time and again, Henry was called away from the farm to repair **steam engines**. One day, on a trip to a Detroit factory, he saw a new type of engine that had been invented by German **engineer** Nikolaus August Otto (1832–91). The engine was powered by gasoline, not steam. It was an **internal combustion engine**—it made its power from gas expanding inside a **cylinder.**

Karl Benz's 1886 tricycle was the world's first successful gasoline-driven car. It reached a speed of about nine mph (14.5 kph).

The new engine was smaller and lighter than the steam engines Henry was used to. It also needed **electricity,** which he knew little about. Back home in Dearborn, Henry explained to Clara what he had seen. He wondered if it would be possible to mount the internal combustion engine on wheels and use it to move a vehicle along. Henry had to find out!

Henry Ford (circled) stands with fellow workers in the engine room of the Edison Illuminating Company, Detroit, about 1895.

But first he had to learn about electricity, and that meant leaving the farm and moving to Detroit. In 1891, Henry began working for the Edison **Illuminating** Company. Once he learned about electricity, Henry's life began a new chapter in his fascination with "automotive transportation."

The light of the future

During the 1890s, the Edison Illuminating Company was one of the most modern businesses in the United States. Just twelve years before Henry Ford joined the firm, its founder, Thomas Edison (1847–1931), had made one of the greatest breakthroughs in science when he invented the electric light bulb. Detroit's homes, businesses, and streets were lit with the "light of the future."

1896: A Car Is Born

O ne year stands out as a **milestone** in the life of Henry Ford. That year was 1896, and it is the year the first Ford motor car was built.

Clara, in 1894, holds her only child, Edsel Ford (1893–1943).

Until that year, Ford's life had been filled with an assortment of unrelated interests and skills. His family had taught him about the hard, manual life of farming. His love of machines had led him to train as an **engineer.** And he had learned about the new science of **electricity.** In 1896, all of these interests came together, like the pieces of a jigsaw puzzle.

Workshops at work and home

As chief engineer for the Edison **Illuminating** Company, Ford had a secure spot in an exciting new industry. His job brought him into contact with other like-minded engineers, people who felt that the new **technology** could be used to bring about great change.

At work, Ford had his own private workshop. During the early 1890s, it was there that he began his experiments in building gasoline-driven **internal combustion engines.** Ford's plan was to make a vehicle for the road. He transferred his experiments to the family home at 58 Bagley Avenue. Here, at the back of the house, was a small brick outbuilding, a former coal shed, which became the center of his car-making activities. Ford did not work alone in his home workshop. Rather, he was helped by friends and colleagues who shared his vision. Each of these people brought skills in such areas as metal-working, electricity, and **fuel supply.** Another important member of the team was Clara Ford, whom Henry affectionately called "The Believer." Clara took his ideas seriously, certain he was about to invent something sensational. When asked by visitors what her husband was working on, she replied, "Henry is making something, and maybe some day I'll tell you."

This reconstruction shows Ford's workshop at 58 Bagley Avenue, Detroit.

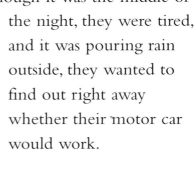

When he was older, Ford would recall his early days with motor cars: "[I dreamed of making] some kind of a light steam car that would take the place of horses … especially as a tractor to attend to the excessively hard labor of plowing. It occurred to me … that precisely the same idea might be applied to a carriage or wagon on the road … but the idea of the carriage at first did not seem so practical to me as the idea of an engine to do the harder farm work."

THE QUADRICYCLE

Ford driving the Quadricycle in 1896. In Detroit, he became known as "Crazy Ford."

In 1896, after almost three years of work, the vehicle created in the Bagley Avenue workshop was finally finished. They called it the Quadricycle because it looked like two bicycles side by side. The team was incredibly exited. Even though it was the middle of the night, they were tired, and it was pouring rain outside, they wanted to find out right away whether their motor car would work.

But the Quadricycle was too big to go through the door! And so, at about 3:00 that morning, Henry took an axe and knocked down part of the wall of the workshop. When Clara heard the

Quadricycle facts

Maximum power	4 horse power (many modern cars have about 100 hp)
Length	6 feet, 5 inches (.50 meter)
Top speed	20 mph (32 kph)
Brakes	none
Weight	500 lbs. (226 kilograms)

commotion, she rushed outside. To her amazement, Ford had started the gasoline engine, climbed into the saddle, held on to the **steering tiller,** and driven out into the night's rain.

Ford took the Quadricycle for a test drive, moving slowly along the streets of Detroit. Jim Bishop, one of the **engineers** who had helped build the car, escorted the noisy vehicle, riding ahead of it on a bicycle.

Toward the end of 1896, Ford was introduced to his hero and employer, Thomas Edison, the founder of the Edison **Illuminating** Company. It was a turning point in Ford's life. Edison was impressed with Ford's gasoline-driven car. He said, "Young man, that's the thing! Your car is self-contained—it carries its own power plant—no fire, no boiler, no smoke, no steam. You have the thing. Keep at it!"

Ford Goes into Business

Ford's thoughts soon turned toward making cars by the hundreds. He was sure it could be done, and, more importantly, he was convinced the public would buy them. But making and selling cars meant setting up a company. That required a lot of money, which Ford didn't have.

After driving the Quadricycle for 1,000 miles (1,689 kilometers), Ford sold it for $200 to Charles Ainsley, the first-ever customer for a Ford motor car. Even though Ford had not built the Quadricycle to sell but rather as an **experimental vehicle,** the money from the sale helped Ford to plan his next step.

The Detroit Automobile Company: 1899 to 1900

Henry Ford was not the only person in America who wanted to create a successful car-making business. By 1899, there were already 80 factories across the country making cars. Other people had seen the future, too.

Ford faced a difficult decision, especially because he had a family to support. "I had to choose between my job and my **automobile,**" he said later. He chose his automobile, and in July of that year Ford went into **partnership** with several wealthy local businessmen. It was their money that led to the founding of the Detroit Automobile Company. Ford resigned from the Edison **Illuminating** Company and went to work full-time at the new car company, taking a risky cut in pay. Ford's job was to oversee the production of the company's car, whatever it was to be.

The plan was to have the first cars ready for sale by October 1899—just three months after the company was set up. But this never happened because although Ford was a genius, he had a lot to learn about working with other people. Convinced that he was always right, Ford wouldn't listen to the advice of his business partners and employees. As a result, fewer than twelve vehicles were made in the first fifteen months.

The company was losing money for its owners, so it was closed down in November 1900. Its materials, parts, and equipment were sold for scrap. Henry was fired by his partners at a meeting he could not bring himself to attend. "If they ask for me," he told a colleague, "tell them I have gone out of town." Without a job, Henry could no longer afford to keep a home, and the family had to move in with Henry's father in Detroit.

The Henry Ford Company:
1901 to 1902

But Ford soon found other businessmen to support him financially, and another new company was set up. It was called the Henry Ford Company, and Ford was its chief **engineer.** The owners thought they were in business to make small cars, but, determined as ever, Ford had a different idea.

These men were the original Ford Motor Company investors.

Ford intended to make racing cars! The owners were furious when they found out, and a few months later Ford was paid $900 to leave the company that bore his name. Its owners continued

Henry Ford steers his first Ford racer in 1901. That year, Ford became the American car-racing champion.

without him, with great success. They changed the company name to the Cadillac Automobile Company. Today, this company is part of General Motors, the world's largest car manufacturer.

Ford's dismissal

Years later, in Henry's rather different version of events about being fired from the Henry Ford Company, he said that it was the directors who had wanted to build racing cars, and Henry who had been interested only in building popular, low-priced cars.

SUCCESS, AT LAST!

The failure of the Detroit **Automobile** Company and his departure from the Henry Ford Company didn't discourage Ford from dreaming of one day having his own car-making business. But until that happened, Ford decided to pursue his new interest in racing cars.

A RACE TO THE FUTURE

The first years of the 1900s were a time of of peace, prosperity, and progress. A new sport, motor racing, was born at around this time, too. Everyone wanted to know, "How fast can a car go?"

The public was fascinated by the sight of cars racing at speeds approaching 40 mph (64 kph). Ford saw this as his opportunity to return to car-making. With money from yet another new **backer**, Ford built two racers, both 10 feet (3 meters) in length. One, called *Arrow,* was painted yellow. The other, called *999,* was red. Both cars were named after high-speed steam trains. Despite the fact that Henry had never raced before, he drove the *Arrow* in a 1901 race against the leading American car-maker Alexander Winton, watched by a crowd of 8,000. "The people went wild," Clara remembered, as Ford's racer roared home the winner.

"The roar of those cylinders at full speed was enough to half kill a man," said Henry. "Going over Niagara Falls would have been a pastime after a ride in the 999."

This painting by H.C. McBarron shows Barney Oldfield's 1902 victory.

Of the two racers, the *999* was chosen to enter a 5-mile (8-kilometer) race against the cars of several car-makers. In October 1902, Ford's 999 racer, driven by Barney Oldfield, a former racing cyclist, set a new American land-speed record of 5 minutes 28 seconds for the distance. This was a little more than a mile (1.6 kilometers) a minute.

The Ford Motor Company: 1903 to the Present

Between 1902 and 1908, no fewer than 502 automobile companies were formed in the United States. Yet again, Ford found himself searching for a wealthy **backer** to set him up in business. Without financial help, Ford's ideas would mean nothing.

Despite Henry's reputation for arrogance and stubbornness, he lucked out again. In 1902, Alex Malcomson, a wealthy coal merchant from Detroit, became

The original share certificate for Henry Ford's initial investment in his motor company.

Ford's latest partner. Their plan was to build a passenger car, and the result was a vehicle they called the Ford Model A. Although it looked just like the cars being made by many other makers, its appearance was deceiving. Ford and his team had used Ford's knowledge of racing cars to improve the Model A's engine. It was more powerful than that of other cars, and the development marked a turning point for Henry Ford. On June 16, 1903, Ford, Malcomson, and their partners established the Ford Motor Company. The car they pinned their hopes on was the Ford Model A.

If the car was a success, perhaps the new company stood a chance of not only surviving, but of emerging as the nation's leading car-maker.

"THE MOST PERFECT MACHINE ON THE MARKET"

The Ford Model A was indeed a success. In July 1903, Dr. E. Pfennig, a dentist from Chicago, became the first person to buy a Ford Model A. It cost him $850. The Ford Model A was billed as "the most perfect machine on the market," and orders came to the Detroit factory from all over the United States. Within eight months, 658 cars had been sold, and by the end of 1904, the company's **output** had reached 1,700 vehicles. Henry Ford had found success as a car-maker at last.

Making a Car, the Early Method

A car factory today is a highly **automated** place to work. Cars are built inside clean, well-lit buildings, where **conveyor belts** move car parts along at a steady rate. The parts are assembled by computerized machines and human workers. This is very different from the car factories of a century ago, like those in which the first Fords were made.

When cars were built by hand

Like many other **manufacturing industries** of the time—such as those that made bicycles, locomotives, and ships—car-makers built their vehicles by hand, one at a time. In the beginning, the Ford Motor Company worked this way, too. The basic component was the car **chassis,** which usually stood on one spot until the car was finished. Parts were carried to the chassis to be fixed in place, like assembling a giant three-dimensional jigsaw puzzle.

Notable Fords: 1903 to 1908

Early Ford cars were named after letters of the alphabet.

Ford	Price	Top speed	Date
Model A	$850	30 mph (48 kph)	1903
Model B	$2,000	40 mph (64 kph)	1904
Model C	$1,000	38 mph (61 kph)	1904
Model F	$1,200	35 mph (56 kph)	1905
Model K	$2,500–$2,800	60 mph (97 kph)	1905
Model N	$600	45 mph (72 kph)	1905
Model R	$750	45 mph (72 kph)	1907
Model S	$700	45 mph (72 kph)	1907
Model T	$260–$850	42 mph (68 kph)	1908

Clara Ford drives
a Model N past
the Ford
Motor Company's
Piquette Avenue
plant in 1905.

An inefficient method

Even after cars were assembled on stands that could
be moved from one team of workers to the next,
the process was still time-consuming and therefore
expensive. If Henry Ford's grand idea of building
cars that ordinary people could afford was ever
going to happen, then a new method of making cars
was essential.

Henry Ford with
his son, Edsel,
aged 12, aboard
a Model F
in 1905.

Glory Days— the Model T Story

Of all the different cars built by Henry Ford, one became a legend. This was the Ford Model T, and it was this car more than any other that fulfilled Ford's dream of making cars affordable for ordinary people. It revolutionized the automobile industry.

For Henry, the early years of the Ford Motor Company were like a voyage of discovery. However, his method of working by instinct frustrated his colleagues. He couldn't read an engineering drawing, so he would hold a part in his hands to tell if it was well designed! Only some of the cars built between 1903 and 1908 were successful. The expensive Ford Model K sold at a loss, and almost put the company out of business.

By 1914, the car was no longer available in red, blue, green, or gray. Ford, who wanted to streamline the production process, said, "you could have any color so long as it is black."

But with each new model built, Ford tried to improve on the preceding one. Learning from his successes and his failures, Ford was moving ever closer to making a world-class car.

A NEW METAL FROM EUROPE

Henry Ford learned from other car-makers, too. In 1905, Henry was at a race when a car from a French company crashed. Pieces of its steel were strewn across the racetrack. Ford picked up a piece. It was lighter and stronger than the metal he used to build his cars, and he wanted it. "That is the kind of material we ought to have in our cars," he said.

Ford found a U.S. company to make the lightweight metal, which was called **vanadium steel.** In 1907, he began using it for his cars, starting with the Ford Model N. The new steel improved the quality of Ford cars, making them lighter and stronger than before. But Ford felt he could make things even better. He wanted to make a car that was lightweight, strong, reliable, and, most of all, inexpensive.

"I will build a car for the great multitude. It will be large enough for the family but small enough for the individual to run and care for. It will be constructed of the best materials… it will be so low in price that no man making a good salary will be unable to own one."

Henry Ford in 1907

"A CAR FOR THE GREAT MULTITUDE"

For an entire year, Ford and his team of **designers** and **engineers** planned the new car. The car was called the Ford Model T, and it was to be made from **vanadium steel.** The project was complicated, and the team found themselves doing things no other car-makers had even tried before. Ford brought his mother's old rocking chair from the farmhouse and sat with the engineers as they worked. Some of the team thought the car might not stand up to everyday use, but Ford was convinced it would. A tough man to work for, Ford inspected every detail of the new design. He insisted on getting small things absolutely right. Ford was determined to create the world's best car.

"It plowed the field
that afternoon,
And when the job
was through
It hummed a pleasant
little tune
And churned the
butter, too."
part of a 1917 song
about the multiple uses
of a Ford Model T engine

A RECORD-BREAKER

The first Ford Model T was sold in 1908 for $850—as much as a teacher earned in a year then. A year later, 10,000 Model Ts had been sold, and the price came tumbling down. In 1916 it cost $345. By 1925 the car cost just $260, a price within the reach of most working people. But Henry had built far more than just an affordable car. Most roads outside towns and cities at that time were rough and unsurfaced. Breakdowns were inconvenient and expensive. Henry made sure that the Model T was a rugged car that could not only cope with such conditions better than any other car, but could even drive over dug-up fields and double as a tractor. Its simple engine design meant that a farmer, or anyone else with basic mechanical knowledge, could repair it easily.

The Ford Model T broke many records. By the time the last one rolled off the production line in December 1927, some 16.5 million "'Tin Lizzies," as they were affectionately known, had been made.

During the early 1920s, Model Ts were also made in England, Ireland, France, Spain, Italy, Germany, Denmark, and Belgium. Henry Ford had put the world on wheels with a car that was described as "useful as a pair of shoes."

The Ford Model T was a "universal car" that could be adapted to suit many different purposes. An example is the 1911 "Ford Express," shown here.

MASS PRODUCTION

A story was told about a Ford factory worker: he dropped his **wrench,** and by the time he'd picked it up he was sixteen cars behind! It was only a joke—and Ford, always fond of a good joke himself, repeated it on a visit with President Woodrow Wilson. The comment illustrates how fast the Model T car-makers worked. The Model T was the result of a method of working called **mass production**. This method enabled Henry Ford to make so many cars, so quickly, and so cheaply.

Women assemble magnetos in a Ford factory in 1913. Female factory workers did not receive the $5 per day minimum wage until 1916.

THE ASSEMBLY LINE

Ford introduced two key processes at his Detroit factory. First, he saved money by making many of the parts at the factory, instead of paying high prices to buy them elsewhere. Second, Ford introduced the moving **assembly line.** Instead of workers walking from car to car, the partially assembled cars were brought to them. They stood at work benches as the parts moved along on chains and **conveyor belts.**

"Every time I reduce the charge for our car by one dollar, I get a thousand new buyers."

Henry Ford

Each worker did one specific job. As Henry Ford said, "The man who puts in a bolt does not put on the nut; the man who puts on the nut does not tighten it." It was as if factory workers assembled identical kits from the 5,000 pieces that went into making every Ford car. It was repetitive, dull work. So in 1914, to attract new workers and prevent others from quitting their jobs, Ford doubled the daily minimum wage. The "$5 day" for unskilled work was a fortune at the time, and once more Henry Ford made history. Before the assembly-line was introduced, it had taken twelve hours to build one Ford Model T. But with mass production, workers cranked out as many as 8,000 Model Ts in a day.

With the assembly-line method, a new Model T left the factory every ten seconds.

FORD THE IDEALIST

The worldwide success of the Ford Model T and the use of **mass production** had helped make Henry Ford into one of the world's richest, and best-known, people. Other businessmen would have been more than satisfied to have achieved so much in so little time. But not Ford: he was restless, and was always looking for new ways to expand his business.

Henry built Fair Lane, a 56-room mansion by the Rouge River in Dearborn, around 1915.

Ford's methods of making inexpensive cars brought him much more than wealth—he became a celebrity with the power to influence the lives of ordinary people around the world. In 1912, Ford visited his car factories in England and France, and for the first time saw how much in demand his cars were in Europe. He saw something else there, too. To an **astute** person like Ford, the rise of **nationalism** and the buildup of arms suggested that the nations of Europe might be on the brink of going to war with each other, and if that happened, his business would suffer. What could he do to protect it?

Henry Ford realized the importance of Europe as the largest market for cars outside the United States.

THE "PEACE SHIP"

Ford returned to America, determined to find a way of preventing a war in Europe from harming his business empire. When **World War I** began in 1914, Ford knew he had to act. In 1915 he declared that he was ready to pay for a "worldwide campaign for universal peace." How he intended to organize such a grand scheme was another matter—he hadn't figured that out. Henry Ford's idea of making "universal peace" made news headlines, and peace campaigners made contact with him, wondering how they could all work together. At a meeting someone suggested sailing a "Peace Ship" to Europe. Ford liked the idea, since it would gain a huge

Henry Ford (center) was on board the "Peace Ship" in 1915 as it left for its ill-fated mission.

amount of **publicity** for his cause, for himself, and also for his car-making business.

Ford chartered a ship, the *King Oscar II*, which was due to sail from New York to Norway in December 1915. In a moment of rashness, Ford said, "We'll get the boys in the trenches home by Christmas." It was an incredible thing for anyone to say, let alone an American, since the United States was not even in the war in 1915. An American newspaper printed this headline on its front page: "Great War Ends Christmas Day: Ford to Stop It." Another headline called Ford "God's Fool."

As Ford sailed on the *King Oscar II* to Norway, he started having doubts about the wisdom of his mission. The papers were making fun of him, and politicians, including the president of the United States, refused to listen to him. And so, as soon as the so-called "Peace Ship" reached Norway, Ford abandoned his plan and boarded the next ship back to the United States.

World War I didn't end at Christmas 1915 but continued until November 1918. By that time, the United States had become involved. Henry Ford's car factories had started making vehicles for the **war effort.**

FORD THE WOULD-BE POLITICIAN

One of Ford's 1918 campaign posters. Henry hoped he would win the votes of working people because of the freedom his automobile had given them.

Despite his great wealth, money never mattered that much to Henry Ford, the country's first billionaire. According to a story, Ford's wife, Clara, once found a check for $75,000 in his pocket. He'd simply forgotten all about it. What mattered more to Ford than money was the power to influence people. His "Peace Ship" mission had been an attempt at using the power he thought he had, but it had ended in bitter failure.

Ford was not a person to give up easily. He considered other ways to put his power to use, and in 1918 announced that he would run for election to the United States **Senate.**

"HENRY FOR SENATOR"

Ford had no real experience of **politics.** He was, after all, a middle-aged wealthy businessman who had spent his working life building up a car-making business. But, as the man who had made cars affordable to all, he was one

Vote for
HENRY FORD
For Senator

The Workingman's Friend

of the best-known people in America. It was this popularity that he hoped would get him elected as a U.S. senator.

At first, things went well for Henry Ford. Farmers, who loved the freedom his cars had brought them, voted for him. Others supported him because of his wartime stand for peace. However, politics is full of traps, and there was danger ahead for Ford.

Ford's opponents ridiculed him for his failed "Peace Ship" mission. Then his son, Edsel, was dragged into the political campaign. Even though he was old enough to fight during the war, Edsel had avoided it. Ford's political enemies accused Edsel of **"draft dodging,"** basically calling him a coward.

A BAD LOSER

Ford's political fate lay in the hands of the voters. It was a close contest, and the votes were counted twice. Ford lost by a narrow margin, and he was angry. He accused his opponent, Truman Newberry, of cheating. Ford claimed that Newberry had spent more money on his **election campaign** than was allowed under the rules. What was worse, Ford claimed that Newberry was controlled by "an influential gang of Jews." This remark revealed a racist side to Henry Ford, which angered many people.

FORD THE EXTREMIST

Two things happened to Henry Ford in November 1918. First, he failed in his attempt to be elected to the U.S. **Senate.** Second, he bought himself a newspaper company. As a senator, Ford would have represented the people who had voted for him. He would have been their official voice in Washington, and his thoughts and opinions would have been reported in newspapers and on radio stations all across the country. But because Ford failed to be elected, he looked for another way to make himself heard.

The Ford International Weekly

THE DEARBORN INDEPENDENT

By the Year $1.50   Dearborn, Michigan, August 6, 1921   Ten Cents

And Now Leprosy Is Yielding to Science
Years of experimenting brings a remedy

Fountain Lake, the Home of John Muir
A story of naturalist's wilderness abode

Fighting the Devil in Modern Babylon
First of a series of articles on New York by Rev. Dr. John Roach Straton

Jewish Jazz—Moron Music—Becomes Our National Music
Story of "Popular Song" Control in the United States

The Chief Justices of the Supreme Court
Only ten men have held this post since the tribunal was first organized

Teaching the Deaf to Hear With Their Eyes
How Chicago is educating afflicted children

Many By-Products From Sweet Potatoes
Recent discoveries prove great possibilities

THE *Dearborn Independent*

Ford chose not to buy a well-known national paper. Instead, he bought his own small-town, local newspaper, the *Dearborn Independent*. The paper was read by people in Dearborn, but was unheard of elsewhere in the country. Ford's ambitious plan was to make it into a major newspaper that would be read from coast to coast across America. Through his paper, Ford would "speak" to the people of America. He would write about the things he believed in, and as the owner of the paper, he could print more or less anything he wanted.

Some of the things he believed were deeply offensive to many people. In 1920, the *Dearborn Independent* printed a stream of anti-Jewish stories. Henry Ford's **extremist views** further exposed him as a **racist.** Meanwhile, Jews were working for him in his car factories.

An end to Ford's paper

In 1924, the *Dearborn Independent* printed a story attacking a Jewish lawyer named Aaron Sapiro. The paper said Sapiro had cheated farmers out of a lot of money, which was untrue. Sapiro took the paper and its owner, Henry Ford, to court. But the case never got that far, because in 1927 Ford apologized to Sapiro and to all Jewish people. His apology was printed in his own newspaper. Ford's reputation had been damaged because of his outspoken beliefs, and his days as a newspaper owner were ending. At the end of 1927, Ford shut down the *Dearborn Independent*.

A Life on Display

Henry Ford lived much of his life in full view of the public. His cars made him a household name. People lined up to work in his car factories. He was involved in **politics.** And he made his beliefs—right or wrong—known through his newspaper. But there was so much more to Ford than most people could possibly know.

Henry Ford, philanthropist

As America's wealthiest man, Henry could afford to be generous. Rather than donate a large sum of money to a charity and expect people to use it wisely, Ford wanted to make sure his money was used the way he thought best. A good example of this took place in Inkster, a small town where people lived in poor conditions. Many of the people were African-American, and many worked at Ford's car factories.

In 1931, Ford set up a supermarket in Inkster where people could buy low-priced food and clothing. It was one of the first supermarkets in the country. Ford reopened the town school, donated seeds for people's gardens, bought sewing machines, and provided lessons in dressmaking. Ford paid for the town's **electricity** supply. His generosity turned Inkster into a better place, and he hoped his efforts would be an example to other underdeveloped communities in the country.

In 1919, Ford donated $11 million to set up a hospital in Detroit. He said that people should be given the same quality of medical care whether they were rich or poor. In 1936, the Ford family set up the Ford Foundation, a charitable organization that provides money for research and education.

While Henry Ford became involved with politics and philanthropy, his car company was building on its early successes.

COMPETITION MOVES IN

During the late 1920's, other automobile companies were trying to produce their own inexpensive and reliable cars. One such competitor was the General Motors Company, which challenged the Model T. The company offered a wide variety of models, introducing a new design each year. Not wanting to harm his success, Ford continued to make only one car, the Model T. Ford's flagship automobile changed little from year to year.

The greatest thrill in motoring.

FINAL YEARS

In 1919, it was time for Henry Ford to step down as president of the Ford Motor Company. Edsel Ford was the natural and only choice to take over the company, which the Ford family owned outright. In 1919, when Edsel was only 25, Henry stepped down, and Edsel took his place.

TIME AWAY FROM CARS

Ford did not plan to disappear quietly into retirement and old age. He liked walking in the woods, bird-watching, and collecting antiques. He also became so enthusiastic about square dancing that he hired a full-time dance teacher and a band. What's more, during Henry's final years, his mind turned to the past.

Edsel Bryant Ford (1893–1943)

Edsel was Henry and Clara Ford's only child. He grew up surrounded by his father's interest in cars, and was given his first car when he was only eight. There was no such thing as a minimum driving age then, and young Edsel drove himself to and from school. Edsel married Ellie Clay in 1916. Their eldest son, born the following year, was named Henry Ford II.

A Museum at Dearborn

One of Ford's all-time heroes was Thomas Edison, his former employer. In 1929, Ford built a vast museum in Dearborn called the Edison Institute of **Technology,** which was later renamed the Henry Ford Museum. The museum honored the inventor to whom Ford owed so much. His idea was simple: Ford wanted to show people "what really happened in years gone by." He bought and moved old buildings from all over America to his museum. He also moved a shepherd's cottage stone by stone across the Atlantic from England and rebuilt it in Dearborn to show people the sort of humble dwelling their English ancestors might have lived in. From the towns and villages of the United States came old log cabins, inns, a blacksmith's forge, the courthouse where Abraham Lincoln had practiced law, the buildings in which Edison had worked, and even the house in which **electric** light had first been used.

Henry Ford (left) and Thomas Edison lay the cornerstone of the Edison Institute of Technology in 1929.

Ford wanted the museum to tell his own story too, to be a place where children could learn about the things he had done as a child, such as spinning wool, tending crops, and caring for farm animals. Ford believed it was simple tasks like these that had made him the person he was.

THE LEGACY OF HENRY FORD

In 1943, Edsel Ford died of cancer at the age of 49. Henry was then eighty years old, and, although he was in poor health, he took charge of the company

again. He wanted a member of the Ford family to always lead the business, so in 1945 he handed control of the Ford Motor Company to Henry Ford II

The Edsel was launched in 1957. It was a medium-priced car with a high vertical radiator grille that the public apparently didn't like. The Edsel lost the Ford Motor Company $250 million before production was stopped in 1959.

(1917-87), his twenty-eight-year-old grandson.

HENRY FORD DIES

Henry Ford died at the age of eighty-three on Monday, April 7, 1947, at his Dearborn home. He died on a night when the Rouge River burst its banks and flooded the cellars of the house. All **electric** power had been cut off, and the huge house was lit by candles. Ford had lived through the birth of the car, the airplane, electric light and the atomic bomb. Yet, on this night, it wasn't just Henry's life that stopped. It was as if time itself had stopped, recalling simpler days when homes were lit with lamps and candles, when **"automotive transportation"** was just a dream.

This modern Ford car plant is in Valencia, Spain.

Henry Ford's legacy

The company formed by Henry Ford in 1903 has grown into an international business success, with more than 250 million Ford vehicles built to date. Ideas developed by Ford, especially the ones related to mass **production,** are now used by car factories worldwide. Although today, computerized machines do much of the work that was done by people during Ford's time, these factories all use his **moving assembly-line** process.

The Ford Motor Company today

In 1999, the Ford Motor Company was the world's second largest manufacturer of cars and trucks. It employed nearly 400,000 people in more than twenty countries. Henry Ford was named "Businessman of the Century" by *Fortune*, an influential business magazine. The Model T was voted "Car of the Century." Car enthusiasts from around the world voted on the Internet, which Ford's current chairman, William Clay Ford Jr., described as "the moving assembly line of the 21st century."

THE CHANGING VIEW OF HENRY FORD

Historians tell the truth about the past. But sometimes, the truth can be hard to find.

> "I am going to see that no man comes to know me."
> Henry Ford

Henry and Clara are shown with their grandson Henry Ford II at the Henry Ford Museum in 1945.

HENRY FORD: HIS OWN WORDS

The story of Ford's early life was published in 1922 in an "autobiography" called *My Life and Work*. The book, which was actually written by a journalist, became a bestseller. In it, some of the facts of Ford's life were changed. For example, Ford claimed that as a boy he had a workbench in his bedroom where he repaired watches for his neighbors. Ford said his father had forbidden this. Ford said he would sneak from the house late at night, ride off on horseback to collect a watch, then repair it at his workbench. He wanted people to think he had fought against authority all his life. But Ford's sister, Margaret, remembers it differently. "Father never forbade him to repair neighbors' watches," she said. " I never knew of him going out at night to get watches ... there was nothing [in his bedroom] except his dresser and a little stand that he kept trinkets in, and his bed."

How Other People Viewed Ford

In 1977, American writer James Brough wrote a book called *The Ford Dynasty*. His book described Ford as a "merciless employer" who made promises he did not keep. But it also called Ford a true genius whose **assembly-line** techniques changed the world. In 1986, British writer Robert Lacey wrote *Ford: The Man and the Machine*, which describes in great detail how Henry Ford had risen from farm boy to all-American folk hero.

Readers are left to consider the evidence and draw their own conclusions about Henry Ford. As his success as a businessman increased, he became involved with **political** and social issues of the day. He held strong and often misguided views on these issues. Ford was, perhaps, a flawed genius. He was a tough man to work for, but was an enlightened employer who gave jobs to men and women regardless of their race or religion. He banned smoking in his factories and was one of the first employers to hire disabled people. No matter what is written or remembered about Henry Ford, one thing is crystal clear. He was a man with a vision of the future. His vision is lived out in today's real world, where the automobile is part of our everyday lives.

"You cannot learn in any school what the world is going to do next year."

Henry Ford

HENRY FORD—TIMELINE

1863 Henry Ford is born on July 30 to William Ford and
Mary Litogot Ford, in Dearborn, Michigan.

1876 Ford's mother dies. He sees a steam engine traveling
along a road, and his fascination with machines begins.

1879 Ford leaves the family farm and goes to Detroit to work in
the city's machine shops.

1882 He returns home as an engineer and makes plans for his
future.

1886 His father gives him land on which to build his own farm.

1888 Ford marries Clara Bryant, of Greenfield township. They
live on Henry's 80-acre (32 hectare) farm.

1891 Henry returns to Detroit to work as an **engineer** with
the Edison **Illuminating** Company.

1893 Edsel Bryant Ford, the only child of Henry and Clara
Ford, is born.

1896 Ford completes his first car, the Quadricycle, and drives it
through the streets of Detroit.

1899 Ford leaves the Edison Illuminating Company to begin a
career making cars. He is made chief engineer and partner
in the newly formed Detroit Automobile Company.

1900 The Detroit Automobile Company closes.

1901 Ford helps form a new car-making company, the Henry
Ford Company.

1902 Ford leaves the Henry Ford Company, which changes its
name to the Cadillac Automobile Company.

1903 Henry helps form the Ford Motor Company.
The company's first car, the Ford Model A, is produced.

1908	Henry begins making the famous Ford Model T.
1910	A new factory opens, in Highland Park, Detroit. It is designed for **mass production.**
1911	The first overseas Ford car factory is established in Manchester, England.
1913	Ford introduces the first **moving assembly line** at his Highland Park factory.
1914	Ford pays male factory workers $5 for an eight-hour day. (Female workers did not receive this wage until 1916.)
1915	The *King Oscar II*, Ford's "Peace Ship, sails to Norway on a mission to end World War I. The one-millionth Ford car is produced.
1918	Ford fails in his attempt to become elected to the U.S. Senate. He buys the *Dearborn Independent* newspaper.
1919	Ford steps down as president of the Ford Motor Company. His son, Edsel, becomes the company's new president.
1927	Production of the Ford Model T ends. The *Dearborn Independent* closes down.
1929	Ford opens the Edison Institute of **Technology,** a major museum.
1936	Henry and Edsel Ford set up the Ford Foundation, a charitable organization.
1943	Edsel Ford dies of cancer. Henry Ford resumes control of the Ford Motor Company.
1945	Henry Ford II takes charge of the Ford Motor Company.
1947	Henry Ford dies at 83 at Fair Lane, his Dearborn home.
1999	*Fortune* magazine names Henry Ford "Businessman of the Century." The Model T is named "Car of the Century."

GLOSSARY

apprentice person trained by an employer to do a job

assembly line system in which goods are assembled in a certain order by workers or machines

astute good at predicting business developments for one's own profit

automated, automation process in which goods are put together by machines

automobile industry name for the worldwide business that makes automobiles

automotive transportation any type of vehicle that moves along using its own power

backer someone who supports or backs another person, usually by providing them with money

chassis metal frame of a car, to which all the other parts are attached

Civil War (1861-65) war fought between the northern and southern states

conveyor belt wide belt that moves things in a factory

cylinder part inside a car engine in which the pistons move, delivering power to the engine

designer person who decides how a car should look, inside and outside

destiny Someone's future or fate

draft dodging avoiding military service if called to join the military

election campaign time immediately before an election when politicians try to persuade voters to elect them

emigrate to leave one country in order to settle in another country

engineer person who designs machines, or who plans the building of roads and bridges

era certain period of history

experimental vehicle vehicle built to try out new ideas

fledgling newly created; often used to describe a new industry

fuel supply circulation of fuel inside a car engine

horseless carriage early road vehicle that moved without being pulled by horses

illumination to light up; old-fashioned name for electric company or the light it produces

industrialization process in which a country changes over from an economy based on farming to one based on factories and machinery

internal combustion engine automobile engine in which the power is generated by fuel burning inside the engine

magneto machine made with magnets that generated current for the ignition in an automobile engine

manufacturing industry industry that makes products, ranging from needles and pins to automobiles and computers

mass production process by which huge numbers of identical things are made quickly and cheaply

mechanism part of a machine

milestone significant event in a person's life

moving assembly line system in which parts are moved along a line of workers or machines

nationalism movement that supports national independence

output number of products a business makes during a certain period of time

partnership agreement between two or more people to work together

philanthropist person who helps others out of kindness

politics having to do with the government of a country

publicity something that brings a matter to the attention of the public, such as a news story

racist person who treats other people unfairly because of his or her race or religion

registered officially written down for legal purposes

steam engine engine powered by steam

steel strong metal made from iron

steering tiller lever modeled after the steering mechanism on a sailboat used for steering early cars

technology study and use of machinery

vanadium steel grayish metallic element used to make strong, lightweight steel

war effort work of citizens to make or grow things to help their country during a war

World War I war fought in Europe from 1914 to 1918 between the United States, Britain, Japan, and their allies against Germany, Austria-Hungary, and their allies

wrench tool used for gripping and turning metal nuts

MORE BOOKS TO READ

Gourley, Catherine. *Wheels of Time: A Biography of Henry Ford.* Brookfield, Conn.: Millbrook Press, 1997.

Middleton, Haydn. *Henry Ford: America's Carmaker.* New York: Oxford University Press, 1998

INDEX